B is for Beach
an alphabet book

Banana Patch Press
www.bananapatchpress.com

Library of Congress Control Number: 2007934180

ISBN-13: 978-0-9715333-8-7

Printed in Hong Kong

B is for Beach
an alphabet book

by

Dr. Carolan

illustrated by
Joanna F. Carolan

audio CD featuring
Leilani Rivera Low

Acknowledgements

Dr. Carolan would like to thank:
    My wife, Joanna, for her beautiful illustrations, love and support
    My four sons, Sean, Seumas, Brendan and Eamonn
    All of the keiki in my practice.

Joanna Carolan would like to thank:
    My husband, Terry, for his wonderful words, love and sense of humor
    The Banana Patch Studio team: Sheri, Dennis, Jana, Vicki, Naomi,
    Michelle, Angela, Shanelle, Brooks, Erin, Brett, Noel, Joel, Grace, Patty,
    Melissa, Lynn, Anna, Crystal, Patricia, Diana, Alice and Kayle.

They would both like to thank:
    Leilani Rivera Low and Darryl Low
    Ron Pendragon, Pancho Graham and Kirby Keough
    Mary Lardizabal and Tia Lardizabal
    Brittany Garces, Anuhea Panui, Kehau Relacion, Catherine Taylan
    Corah Callahan, Kjan Forbes-Vink and Kalea Hui-hui-Caberto
    Tom Niblick at The Printmaker in Lihue.

For Eva, Kjan and Kelly

A a

A is for Aloha.
In Hawai'i, "Aloha" is what you say
For "Hello" or "Good-bye" or
"Have a nice day!"

B is for Beach.

Hawaii's beaches are lots of fun.
You can swim or surf,
Or just lie in the sun.

C c

C is for Coconut.

Coconuts are good to eat,
But picking them off the tree
Is a difficult feat.

D d

(duck, dinosaur, dog, diver, dragonfly, dinghy, diamond, dock, drink)

D is for Dolphin.
Look closely and you will see
Many other things
That begin with "D".

E e

E is for Elephant.
In Hawai'i there are none;
If there were elephants here,
Wouldn't it be fun!

F f

F is for Flowers.
Hawaii's flowers are a beautiful sight.
They come in all colors,
Pink, yellow, orange, red and white.

G g

G is for Gecko.

Geckos have toes that are sticky,
So they can climb up walls
To eat the bugs that are icky!

H is for Hawai'i.

With miles of ocean on every side,
The beautiful islands of Hawai'i
Are known far and wide.

H h

I is for Ice Cream.

Eat it in a cone or with a spoon,
Ice cream is good either way
As long as we get some soon!

J j

J is for Jellyfish.
Not a fish, they are more of a thing:
Jellyfish have no eyes, ears or brains,
But watch out for their sting!

K k

K is for Kayak.
Kayaks are a fun kind of a boat.
Even if you turn them over,
They will still stay afloat.

L l

L is for Lei.
A flower lei is nice to wear.
Making someone a lei
Shows them that you care.

M m

M is for Moon.
Hawai'i is beautiful in the moonlight.
It seems that here
The moon shines especially bright.

N n

N is for Nene.

The nene is the Hawaiian goose.
And to make a rhyme for nene
I'd need to be Dr. Seuss.

O o

O is for Outrigger.

An outrigger canoe is fun to ride.
The outrigger keeps the canoe
From tipping on its side.

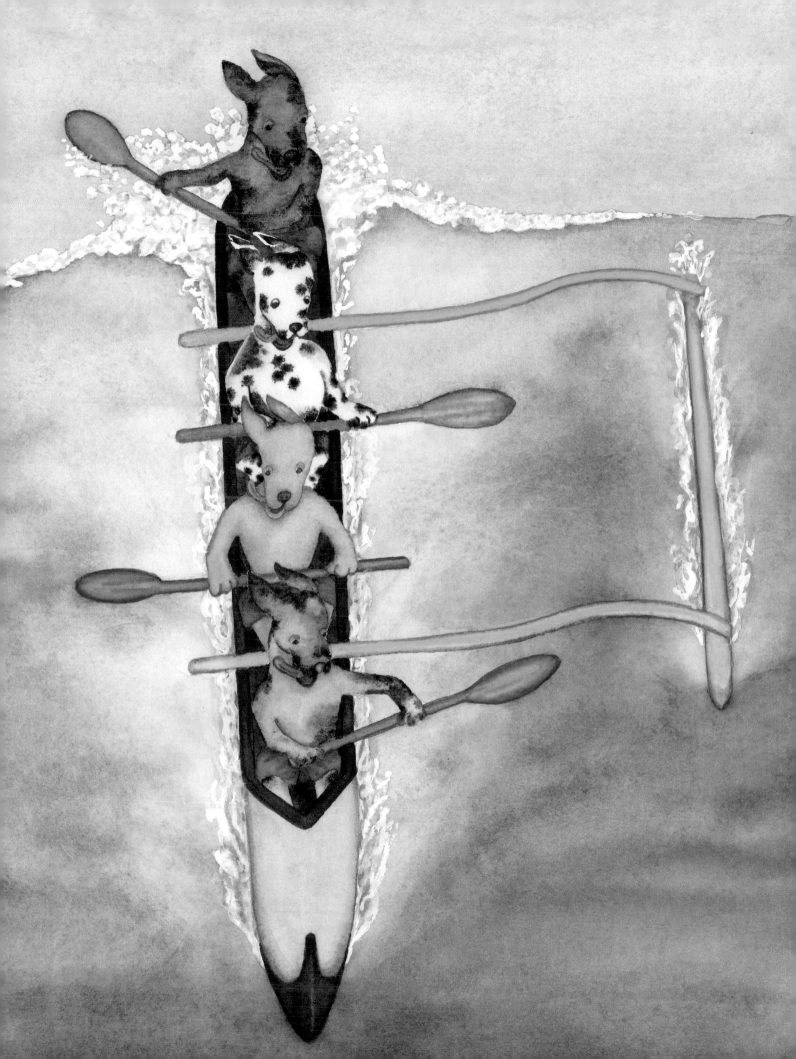

P p

P is for Papaya.
Papayas are delicious any time.
Have one for breakfast,
With a slice of lime.

Q q

Q is for Quilt.
Hawaiian quilts are nice and bright.
They come in many patterns,
And keep you warm at night.

R is for Rainbow.

Rainbows are made by rain and sun.
You need them both,
Or you won't ever see one.

S s

S is for Surfing.
Catching a wave is really a thrill.
It is not as easy as it looks,
Surfing takes practice and skill.

T t

T is for Turtle.

Hawaii's turtles live in the sea
But they breathe air
Just like you and me.

U u

U is for 'Ukulele.
As the hula dancer sways and sings,
The musicians beat the drums
And play the 'ukulele strings.

V is for Volcano.

The volcano is starting to blow!
See the smoke, rocks, ashes,
And red hot lava flow.

W w

W is for Whale.

Whales swim to Hawai'i each year.
They have their babies
In the warm ocean here.

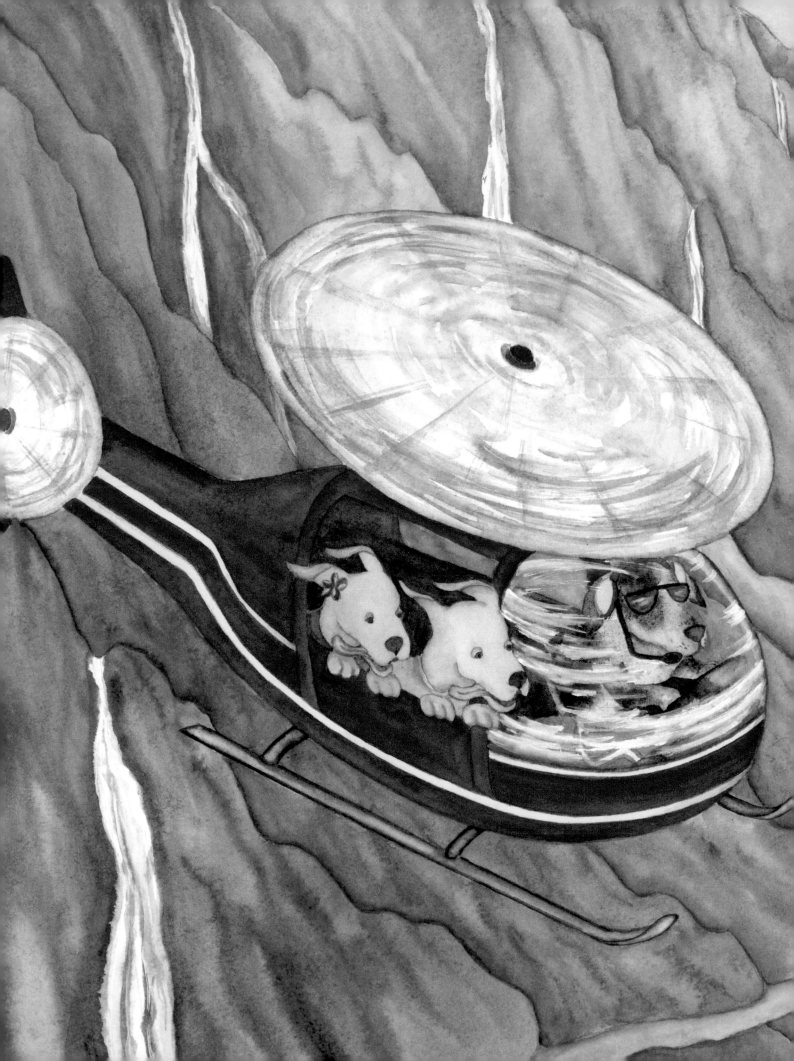

X x

X is for eXciting.
It's exciting to do something new
Like riding in a helicopter
And taking in the view!

Y y

Y is for Yacht.
Look through the coconut trees,
See all the yachts
Sailing in the tropical breeze.

Z is for Zori.

At the Honolulu zoo I lost a zori.
Where did I find it?
Well, that's another story...

Now let's sing the alphabet song.
We will begin,
And you sing along.
(Sung to the tune of *Twinkle, Twinkle Little Star*)

Ho'omākaukau   *(Get Ready)*
Pa *(Start)*

Now let us try something new.
The Hawaiian letters are just a few:
A, E, I, O me U   *(A, E, I, O and U)*
H, K, L, M me N   *(H, K, L, M and N)*
P me W, and now we're done.   *(P and W)*
Learning your letters is lots of fun!

Come and sing along with me.
It's easy to learn as you will see:
A, E, I, O me U   (A, E, I, O and U)
H, K, L, M me N   (H, K, L, M and N)
P me W, and now we're done.   (P and W)
Learning your letters is lots of fun!

Maikaʻi!   (Good!)

In the recording studio, Kaua'i, Hawai'i
(L to R): Kehau Relacion, Tia Lardizabal, Brittany Garces,
Catherine Taylan, Anuhea Panui

About the READ ALONG CD:
Read by: Leilani Rivera Low
Guitar & 'Ukulele: Kirby Keough
Slack Key Guitar & Bass: Pancho Graham
ABC Song by: Leilani Rivera Low, Tia Lardizabal, Brittany Garces,
Anuhea Panui, Kehau Relacion, Catherine Taylan
Choir Direction: Mary Lardizabal
Kids voices: Corah Callahan, Kjan Forbes-Vink, Kalea Hui-hui-Caberto

Executive Producer: Banana Patch Press
Producer: Ron Pendragon
Sound Design, Recorded, Mixed & Mastered by:
Ron Pendragon, Kaua'i, Hawai'i
www.fattuesdayrecords.com

LEILANI RIVERA LOW was born and raised in Wailua, Kaua'i. She began entertaining as a young girl, performing nightly with her father Larry Rivera and family at the famed Coco Palms Resort on Kaua'i. She took hula lessons from an early age, and by age 13 was creating and teaching hula to other Coco Palms performers.

Today Leilani is a renowned Kumu Hula, composer and recording artist. She has presented her award-winning music and hula in concerts throughout the Hawaiian Islands, on the mainland, as well as in Japan and Tahiti. For more information visit: www.leilanirivera.com

PANCHO GRAHAM grew up in Kailua and played bass in the youth symphony. He lives on Kaua'i and is a member of the esteemed musical group *Nā Pali*. Graham is a composer, singer, and master of many instruments including guitar, 'ukulele and string bass. For more information visit: www.myspace.com/panchograham

KIRBY KEOUGH has been playing guitar & 'ukulele since his "small kid" days. He was born on Oahu. His mother is Hawaiian and his father is Irish-Norwegian. He has lived on Kaua'i for 30 years where he is a well-known entertainer. For more information email: keoughk001@hawaii.rr.com

DR. CAROLAN was born in Melbourne, Australia. He is a pediatrician in private practice on the island of Kaua'i, Hawai'i. He is married to Joanna F. Carolan.

JOANNA F. CAROLAN was born in San Francisco, California. She is an artist and owner of Banana Patch Studio, an art studio and gallery on Kaua'i.

Other Dr. Carolan books available from Banana Patch Press:

Ten Days in Hawaii, A Counting Book
Where Are My Slippers? A Book of Colors
Goodnight Hawaiian Moon
Old Makana Had a Taro Farm
This is My Piko
A President From Hawai'i
The Magic 'Ukulele

For more information visit:
www.bananapatchpress.com
www.bananapatchstudio.com

O P Q

R S T U

V W X

Y and Z